3/09

WITHDRAWN

WALTZ
WITH
BASHIR

WALTZ WITH BASHIR

A LEBANON WAR STORY

ARI FOLMAN
DAVID POLONSKY

Metropolitan Books
Henry Holt and Company • New York

Metropolitan Books
Henry Holt and Company, LLC
Publishers since 1866
175 Fifth Avenue
New York, New York 10010
www.henryholt.com

Metropolitan Books® and ® are registered trademarks of Henry Holt and Company, LLC.

Library of Congress Cataloging-in-Publication Data

Folman, Ari.
    Waltz with Bashir : a Lebanon war story / Ari Folman, David Polonsky — 1st U.S. ed.
        p. cm.
    ISBN-13: 978-0-8050-8673-7 (hardcover)
    ISBN-10: 0-8050-8673-0 (hardcover)
    ISBN-13: 978-0-8050-8892-2 (pbk.)
    ISBN-10: 0-8050-8892-X (pbk.)
    1. Folman, Ari—Comic books, strips, etc. 2. Soldiers—Israel—Biography—Comic books, strips, etc. 3.
Sabra and Shatila Massacre, Lebanon, 1982—Personal narratives, Israeli—Comic books, strips, etc. 4.
Lebanon—History—Israeli intervention, 1982–1984—Atrocities—Comic books, strips, etc. 5. Graphic
novels. I. Polonsky, David. II. Title.
DS87.53.F65 2008
956.9204'4—dc22   2008023322

Henry Holt books are available for special promotions and premiums.
For details contact: Director, Special Markets.

First U.S. Edition 2009
Printed in China
10 9 8 7 6 5 4 3 2 1

WALTZ
WITH
BASHIR

THE NIGHT BOAZ CALLED WAS THE WORST NIGHT THAT WINTER.
IT WAS JANUARY 2006. NOTHING IN OUR THIRTY YEARS OF FRIENDSHIP
HAD PREPARED ME FOR THE STORY HE WAS ABOUT TO TELL.

THE DOGS HAVE BEEN COMING FOR TWO YEARS, HE SAID.

YOU'LL BE OKAY, RIGHT?

THINK SO?

SURE. I'LL COME UP WITH SOMETHING.

AND NOT JUST FROM LEBANON, BUT FROM WEST BEIRUT.

AND NOT JUST FROM WEST BEIRUT...

...BUT FROM THE NIGHT OF THE MASSACRE...

...IN THE SABRA AND SHATILA REFUGEE CAMPS.

AFTER A NIGHT LIKE THAT THE ONLY THING TO DO WAS GO SEE MY BEST FRIEND ORI.

IS SOMETHING WRONG? IT'S 6:30 IN THE MORNING.

SO? EVERYONE HAS A LAWYER-FRIEND, A DOCTOR-FRIEND AND A SHRINK-FRIEND. SOMETIMES YOU HAVE TO PAY THE PRICE.

BUT YOU WOULDN'T WAKE YOUR LAWYER-FRIEND AT 6:30.

BECAUSE MY LAWYER-FRIEND SAVES ME A WHOLE LOT MORE MONEY THAN YOU DO.

YOU KNOW, THERE'S ONE THING I DON'T UNDERSTAND. WHY DID I NEED BOAZ'S CRAZY DOG DREAM TO JOG MY MEMORY? IT HAD NOTHING TO DO WITH ME.

MEMORY IS A VERY INTERESTING THING. I'LL TELL YOU ABOUT A WELL-KNOWN EXPERIMENT IN PSYCHOLOGY.

THEY SHOWED A GROUP OF PEOPLE PICTURES FROM THEIR CHILDHOOD. MOST PICTURES WERE OF THINGS THAT HAD REALLY HAPPENED.

ONE PICTURE, OF AN AMUSEMENT PARK, WAS PHONY.

THEY PLANTED IMAGES OF THE CHILDREN IN A PHOTO OF THE PARK, WHICH THEY HAD NEVER ACTUALLY VISITED.

EIGHTY PERCENT OF THE PEOPLE SAW THEMSELVES IN THE PHONY PICTURE AND REMEMBERED THE EVENT, EVEN THOUGH IT HAD NEVER HAPPENED.

THE RESEARCHERS TOLD THE OTHER TWENTY PERCENT...

...TO "GO HOME AND THINK ABOUT IT."

WHEN THEY SAW THE PICTURE AGAIN, EACH ONE SAID...

..."YES, I REMEMBER BEING AT THE AMUSEMENT PARK WITH MY PARENTS AND HAVING A WONDERFUL DAY."

MEMORY IS DYNAMIC, IT'S ALIVE.

IF DETAILS ARE MISSING AND THERE ARE SOME BLACK HOLES, MEMORY FILLS IN THE EMPTY SPACES UNTIL IT COMPLETELY "RECALLS" SOMETHING THAT NEVER HAPPENED.

ARE YOU SAYING THAT MY FLASHBACK OF THE MASSACRE NEVER HAPPENED? THAT I INVENTED IT?

I DON'T KNOW. YOU CAN CHECK. WHO WAS THERE WITH YOU?

THERE WAS CARMI, YOU REMEMBER HIM FROM HIGH SCHOOL. HE'S IN HOLLAND NOW. AND THERE'S SOMEONE ELSE WHO I CAN'T PLACE.

SO IF IT REALLY MATTERS TO YOU, GO TO HOLLAND AND ASK CARMI WHAT HE REMEMBERS.

DON'T YOU THINK IT'S DANGEROUS? MAYBE I'LL DISCOVER THINGS ABOUT MYSELF THAT I DON'T WANT TO KNOW.

THERE'S A HUMAN MECHANISM THAT BLOCKS US FROM GOING INTO THE DARK AREAS WE WANT TO KEEP CLOSED.
YOUR MEMORY WILL ONLY TAKE YOU WHERE YOU NEED TO GO.

17

CARMI'S BEEN LIVING IN HOLLAND FOR THE PAST TWENTY YEARS. I'D ALWAYS WANTED TO VISIT HIM BUT SOMEHOW IT NEVER HAPPENED. IT WAS KIND OF WEIRD TO GO THERE AFTER ALL THIS TIME ON THE PRETEXT OF RESEARCHING A FORGOTTEN WAR.

SEE ALL THIS?

IT'S ALL MINE.

FROM THOSE TREES OVER THERE TO THE RIVER ON THE OTHER SIDE. ABOUT TEN ACRES.

ALL THIS FROM SELLING FALAFEL?

YEAH, ALL THIS FROM SELLING FALAFEL.

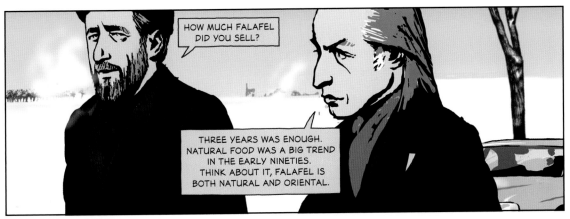

HOW MUCH FALAFEL DID YOU SELL?

THREE YEARS WAS ENOUGH. NATURAL FOOD WAS A BIG TREND IN THE EARLY NINETIES. THINK ABOUT IT, FALAFEL IS BOTH NATURAL AND ORIENTAL.

PEOPLE THOUGHT YOU'D BECOME A PHYSICIST, AN ATOMIC SCIENTIST.

WHAT PEOPLE?

YOU KNOW, MY PARENTS, YOUR PARENTS, THE KIDS AT SCHOOL, EVERYONE.

BY THE TIME I WAS TWENTY, IT WAS OVER. I COULDN'T BECOME ANYTHING.

IT'S FUNNY. JUST BEFORE YOU SHOWED UP, MY SON THOMAS WENT OUT TO PLAY WITH A PLASTIC RIFLE.

WHILE HE WAS PLAYING HE STARTED ASKING QUESTIONS: WHAT DID I DO IN THE ARMY, DID I EVER SHOOT ANYONE?

DID YOU?

I DON'T KNOW.

YOU COLD?

YES, FREEZING.

LET'S GO INSIDE, IT'S WARMER.

AS AMAZING AS IT SOUNDS, WE WENT TO WAR ON A LITTLE BOAT, A KIND OF LOVE BOAT THAT THE ARMY LEASED OR SOMETHING.

THEY DID IT TO MISLEAD THE ENEMY AND SURPRISE THEM BY SEA.

YEARS LATER I HEARD THAT IT WAS JUST A COMMANDO BOAT PAINTED PINK.

YOU KNOW, THERE'S SOMETHING THAT PUZZLES ME. YOU TURNED INTO SUCH A FIGHTER, BUT AT EIGHTEEN YOU SEEMED LIKE A PRETTY ENLIGHTENED KID.

THE TRUTH IS, IT WAS IMPORTANT TO ME FOR A VERY PROSAIC REASON.

I ALWAYS HAD THE FEELING THAT EVERYONE AROUND ME WAS SCREWING LIKE RABBITS WHILE I WAS THE NERD WINNING ALL THE CHESS COMPETITIONS.

I THOUGHT I WAS THE ONLY ONE WITH MASCULINITY PROBLEMS. SO I HAD TO PROVE THAT I WAS A GREAT FIGHTER, A BIG HERO.

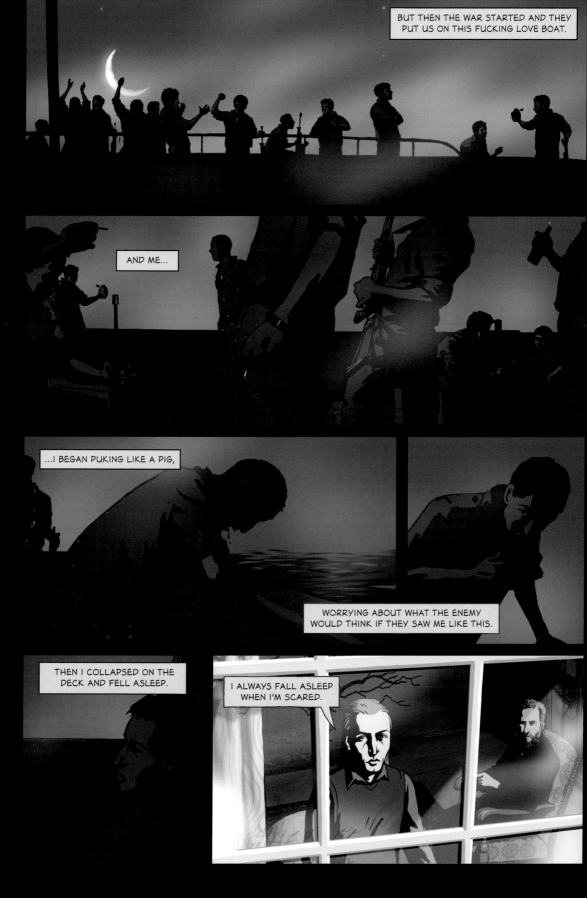

EVEN NOW, I ESCAPE
INTO SLEEP AND FANTASIES.

SO, I'M LYING ON THE DECK, PASSED OUT,

DREAMING THAT FINALLY...

...A WOMAN COMES
ALONG, JUST FOR ME.

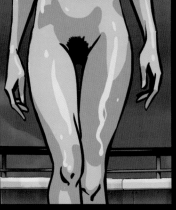

SHE CARRIES ME AWAY...

...AND I GET LAID FOR THE FIRST TIME.

FROM A DISTANCE, I SEE MY FRIENDS...

...GOING UP IN FLAMES...

...RIGHT BEFORE MY EYES.

I WAKE UP JUST BEFORE WE LAND.

23

WHEN WE REACH THE SHORE, IT'S DAYBREAK AND WE'RE GOING INTO THE CITY. I DON'T KNOW WHICH ONE. SIDON, I THINK.

WITH ALL THE PRESSURE AND THE FEAR, WE START SHOOTING LIKE MANIACS. I HAVE NO IDEA AT WHAT.

I SEE A BLUE MERCEDES COMING DOWN THE ROAD AND EVERYONE'S FIRING AT IT LIKE CRAZY.

EVEN AFTER TWO YEARS OF TRAINING, THERE'S NOTHING BUT UNCONTROLLABLE FEAR. AND THEN SILENCE, THE HORRIFIC SILENCE OF DEATH.

WHEN IT'S FULLY LIGHT, YOU SEE THE HAVOC YOU'VE CAUSED.

AND LYING IN THE CAR...

...ARE THE BODIES OF A FAMILY.

TELL ME, WHY DID YOU COME?

I'VE LOST MY MEMORY.

IN AN ACCIDENT? A WORK ACCIDENT?

NO, NO ACCIDENT.

IT'S JUST THE WHOLE PERIOD OF THE LEBANON WAR. I CAN'T REMEMBER ANYTHING. I HAVE JUST ONE IMAGE IN MY MIND FROM THEN AND YOU'RE IN IT, SOMEHOW.

WHAT IMAGE?

WERE YOU WITH ME?

IT'S HARD TO SAY.

WHAT DO YOU MEAN? WERE YOU THERE?

I DON'T KNOW. I CAN'T REMEMBER ANYTHING TO DO WITH THE MASSACRE.

BUT YOU WERE THERE. YOU WERE IN BEIRUT DURING THE MASSACRE.

YES, I REMEMBER BEING IN BEIRUT. THE INVASION WILL BE WITH ME FOR THE REST OF MY LIFE. BUT... HOW CAN I SAY IT? THE MASSACRE'S NOT IN MY SYSTEM.

THEN IT HAPPENED.

IN A TAXI ON THE WAY TO THE AIRPORT IN AMSTERDAM.

SUDDENLY—BOOM!

THE WAR CAME BACK. MY MEMORY BLEW WIDE OPEN.

IT WAS NO HALLUCINATION, NO DREAM, NOTHING SUBCONSCIOUS.

IN THE EVENING WE STOP. AN OFFICER COMES OVER TO US.

YOU—LOAD UP THE DEAD AND THE WOUNDED ON YOUR VEHICLE AND DUMP THEM.

DUMP THEM?

YEAH, DUMP THEM.

DUMP THEM WHERE?

HOW SHOULD I KNOW? LOOK FOR A BRIGHT LIGHT. THAT'S WHERE THEY USUALLY DUMP THE BODIES.

SO I FIND MYSELF GOING BACK THE WAY WE CAME. ME, WHO IN MY WHOLE LIFE HAS HARDLY SEEN A DROP OF BLOOD, LET ALONE AN OPEN WOUND, SUDDENLY I'M COMMANDING AN APC FULL OF INJURED SOLDIERS AND DEAD MEN, LOOKING FOR A BRIGHT LIGHT.

WHAT ARE WE SUPPOSED TO BE DOING? WHY DON'T YOU TELL US WHAT TO DO?

SHOOT.

AT WHAT?

I DON'T KNOW. JUST SHOOT.

ISN'T IT BETTER TO PRAY?

YOU CAN SHOOT AND PRAY.

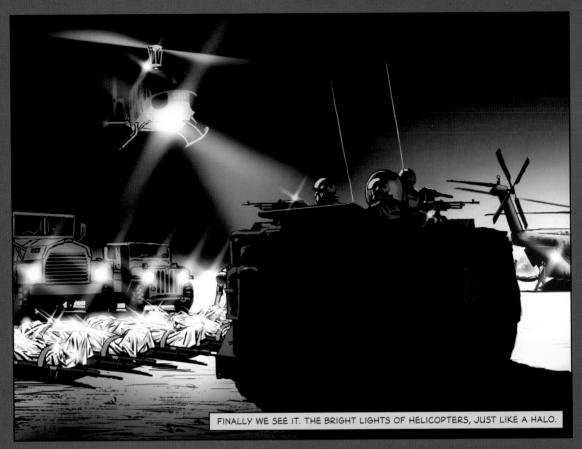

FINALLY WE SEE IT. THE BRIGHT LIGHTS OF HELICOPTERS, JUST LIKE A HALO.

WE APPROACH THE LIGHT.

WHEN WE REACH IT, WE SEE THAT THE PLACE IS FULL OF CORPSES.

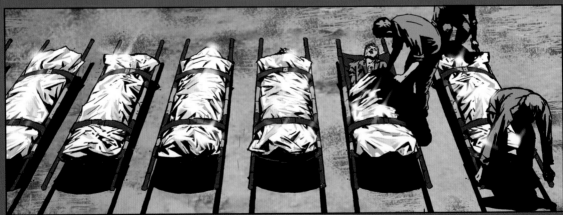

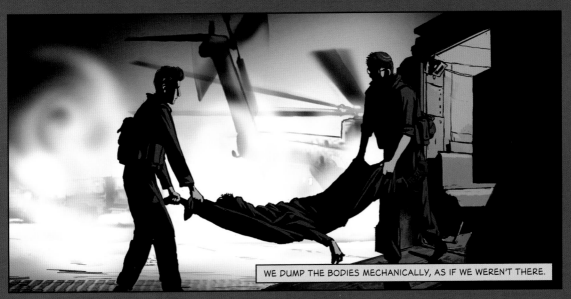

WE DUMP THE BODIES MECHANICALLY, AS IF WE WEREN'T THERE.

WE WASH OUT THE APC, TURN OUR BACKS...

...AND DRIVE AWAY.

I WAS SUPPOSED TO TAKE OVER, BUT AT THAT MOMENT I DIDN'T REACT THE WAY I SHOULD HAVE. WE JUST SAT IN THE TANK. IT DIDN'T OCCUR TO US TO FIRE BACK AT ANYTHING.

A MINUTE OR TWO LATER THERE WAS AN EXPLOSION.

EVERYONE SCRAMBLED TO ESCAPE THE TANK, JUST AS WE WERE, WITHOUT WEAPONS OR ANYTHING.

WHOEVER DIDN'T MANAGE TO GET AWAY WAS KILLED RIGHT THERE.

I RAN LIKE CRAZY, GOING IN ZIGZAGS TOWARD THE SEA.

THE ONLY THOUGHT IN MY HEAD WAS, THAT'S THE END, FOR ME IT'S OVER.

I COULD SEE OUR COMPANY COMMANDER'S TANK. I HOPED SOMEHOW HE'D COME CLOSER. BUT INSTEAD HE STARTED RETREATING. I WAS ALONE.

THERE WAS NOTHING TO DO BUT WAIT FOR THE END.

I THOUGHT ABOUT MY MOTHER AND HOW SHE WOULD REACT. SHE'S VERY ATTACHED TO ME. I'VE ALWAYS BEEN HER RIGHT HAND. I'M THE ONE WHO HELPS OUT AT HOME.

THEN I TOOK A PEEK. I COULD SEE THE PALESTINIANS TALKING, LAUGHING, SMOKING. I WAS SURPRISED THEY WEREN'T LOOKING IN MY DIRECTION. AFTER A WHILE I REALIZED THAT THEY PROBABLY THOUGHT WE'D ALL BEEN KILLED IN THE ATTACK.

I THOUGHT I'D WAIT UNTIL DARK. IT WAS A PRETTY GOOD PLACE TO HIDE.

I DON'T KNOW WHY, BUT WHEN THE EVENING CAME, I DECIDED TO CRAWL TO THE SEA.

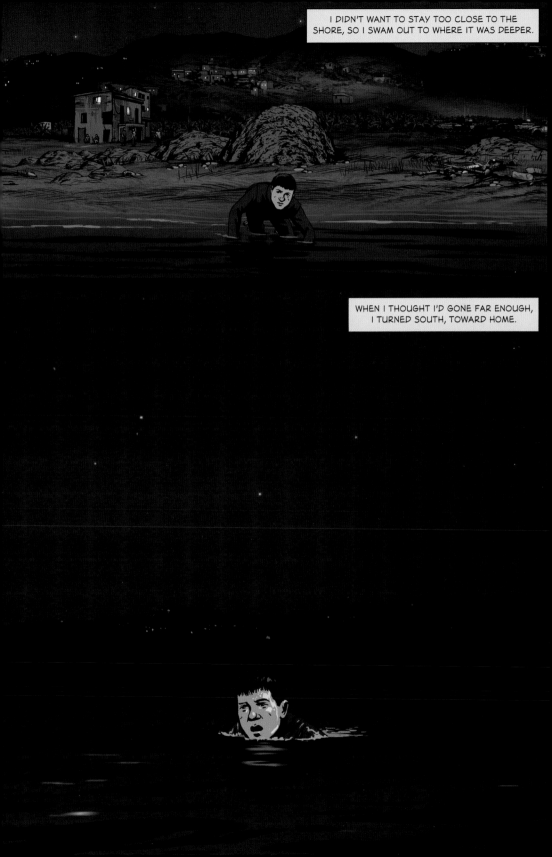

THE WATER WAS VERY QUIET, CALM, THERE WERE HARDLY ANY WAVES. IT WAS JUST ME AND THE SEA.

I FELT A KIND OF PEACE BECAUSE THE SEA WAS SO CALM, LIKE IT WAS ON MY SIDE.

BUT AT THE SAME TIME I WAS TERRIFIED THAT SOMEBODY WOULD SEE ME AND SHOOT ME AND KILL ME. I KEPT SWIMMING IN THE STILLNESS, BUT THEN I BEGAN LOSING MY STRENGTH. I COULDN'T MOVE MY LIMBS.

THERE WERE MOMENTS WHERE I JUST FLOATED AND LET THE WATER CARRY ME.

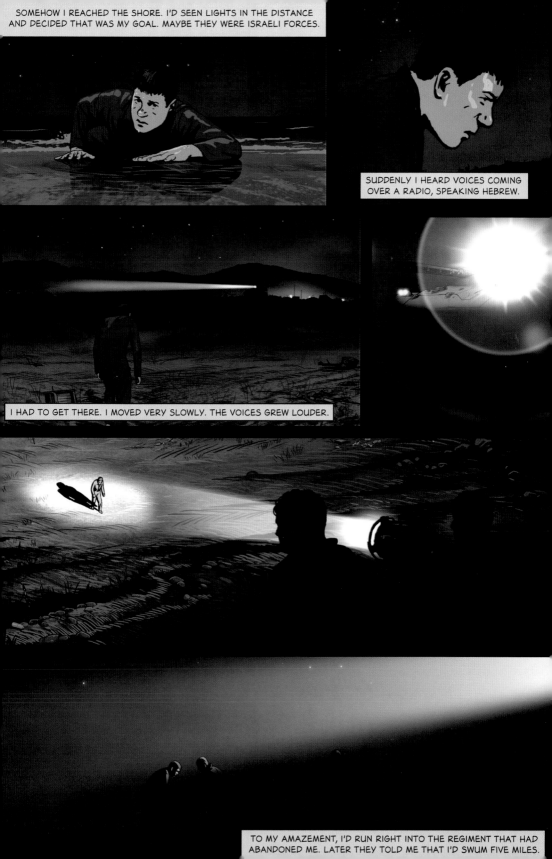

AFTER I REJOINED THEM, I FELT AS IF I'D SOMEHOW ABANDONED THEM. I HAD THE FEELING THEY SAW ME AS SOMEONE WHO'D DESERTED HIS FRIENDS, WHO'D RUN FROM THE BATTLEFIELD TO SAVE HIS OWN SKIN.

I CUT MYSELF OFF FROM MY FRIENDS' FAMILIES. AT FIRST I VISITED THEIR GRAVES, BUT I DIDN'T WANT TO BE THERE. I WANTED TO FORGET.

WHEN YOU GO TO THE CEMETERY, YOU FEEL...GUILTY.

IT'S AS IF I DIDN'T DO ENOUGH. I WASN'T THE KIND OF HERO WHO PULLS OUT HIS WEAPONS AND SAVES EVERYONE.

THAT'S NOT WHO I AM.

A MONTH AFTER RONNIE DAYAG HAD SWUM BACK TO HIS REGIMENT...

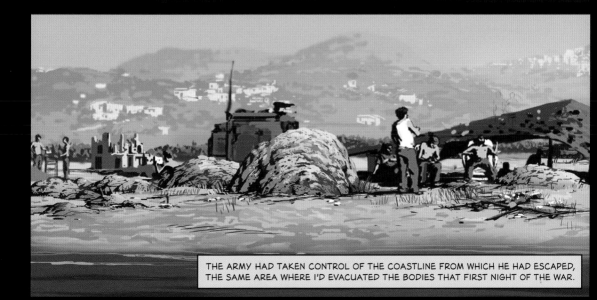

THE ARMY HAD TAKEN CONTROL OF THE COASTLINE FROM WHICH HE HAD ESCAPED,
THE SAME AREA WHERE I'D EVACUATED THE BODIES THAT FIRST NIGHT OF THE WAR.

THEY KEPT TELLING US THAT SOON WE'D INVADE BEIRUT AND WE WERE GOING TO DIE.

BUT WE WERE ALL HANGING OUT, DOWN ON THE BEACH.

AND WE WEREN'T THINKING MUCH ABOUT DEATH.

EVEN THE INCIDENTS OF FRIENDLY FIRE DIDN'T BOTHER US TOO MUCH.

WE WERE KIND OF UNAWARE OF A LOT THAT WAS GOING ON.

I HAD A CABIN MADE OF BANANA LEAVES. WHEN I THINK BACK TO THAT TIME...

...I FEEL DRENCHED ALL OVER WITH THE AWFUL SMELL OF PATCHOULI, A COLOGNE THAT WAS POPULAR IN THE EIGHTIES.

BUT TO MY CABINMATE, FRENKEL, PATCHOULI WASN'T A COLOGNE. IT WAS A WAY OF LIFE.

SO, THE DAILY ROUTINE BACK THEN: WE'D GET UP IN THE MORNING.

WE FIXED OUR BREAKFAST RIGHT THERE ON THE BEACH, CANNED BEEF AND EGGS.

THE ORDER WOULD COME DOWN:

SEND OUT THE MEN.

GET YOUR GEAR...

...PUT ON YOUR FLAK JACKETS...

...AND GO HUNT FOR TERRORISTS.

WE WERE DOWN ON THE GROUND.

I HEARD SOMEONE YELL, "FRENKEL!"

THROUGH THE TREES I SAW A BOY STANDING THERE, A BOY WITH AN RPG.

HE WAS A YOUNG BOY.

FRENKEL, TELL ME, WAS I THERE?

WHAT DO YOU MEAN, WERE YOU THERE? WHEREVER I WENT, YOU WENT WITH ME.

OF COURSE YOU WERE THERE.

GOOD TO KNOW. YES, YES, OF COURSE I WAS THERE.

PROFESSOR ZEHAVA SOLOMON IS A WORLD EXPERT ON COMBAT TRAUMA. IF ANYONE COULD EXPLAIN THE BLANKS IN MY MIND, SHE COULD.

TELL ME, HOW COULD I HAVE BEEN INVOLVED IN SOMETHING LIKE AN RPG ATTACK AND HAVE ABSOLUTELY NO MEMORY OF IT?

THAT'S WHAT WE CALL A "DISSOCIATIVE EVENT." IT HAPPENS WHEN A PERSON IS IN A CERTAIN SITUATION BUT FEELS LIKE HE'S OUTSIDE OF IT.

YOU'RE NOT THE ONLY ONE. THERE WAS A YOUNG MAN, A PHOTOGRAPHER. IN '83 I ASKED HIM, HOW DID YOU GET THROUGH SUCH A NIGHTMARE? HE SAID, IT WAS PRETTY EASY. I TRIED TO PRETEND I WAS ON A TRIP.

HE KEPT THINKING HE WAS SEEING IT THROUGH THE LENS OF AN IMAGINARY CAMERA.

HE TOLD HIMSELF, WOW, THESE ARE AMAZING SCENES. THERE'S SHOOTING, SCREAMING, EXPLOSIONS, PEOPLE WOUNDED.

UNTIL SOMETHING HAPPENED AND IT
WAS AS IF HIS CAMERA HAD BROKEN.

HE SAID, "LOOK, IT WAS A REALLY TERRIBLE MOMENT. WE GOT TO THE HIPPODROME IN BEIRUT, WHERE THE STABLES WERE...

...AND I SAW ALL THESE BODIES, THESE CORPSES OF BEAUTIFUL ARABIAN HORSES. THEY'D BEEN SLAUGHTERED. IT BROKE MY HEART."

"WAR IS BAD ENOUGH, THE THINGS PEOPLE DO TO EACH OTHER", HE TOLD ME, "BUT WHAT HAD THESE LOVELY HORSES DONE, WHAT SIN HAD THEY COMMITTED, THAT THEY HAD TO SUFFER THIS WAY?"

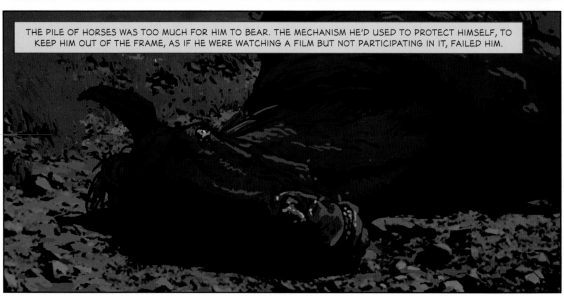

THE PILE OF HORSES WAS TOO MUCH FOR HIM TO BEAR. THE MECHANISM HE'D USED TO PROTECT HIMSELF, TO KEEP HIM OUT OF THE FRAME, AS IF HE WERE WATCHING A FILM BUT NOT PARTICIPATING IN IT, FAILED HIM.

HE HAD BEEN PULLED INTO THE PICTURE, AND THEN HE LOST HIS MIND.

YOU SAID YOU DON'T REMEMBER BEING IN THE ORCHARD WITH THE RPG KID. DO YOU REMEMBER OTHER THINGS FROM THAT PERIOD?

YES, I REMEMBER MY HOME LEAVE IN DETAIL.

WHEN I CAME HOME FROM LEBANON FOR THE FIRST TIME IN SIX WEEKS, LIFE WAS GOING ON AS NORMAL.

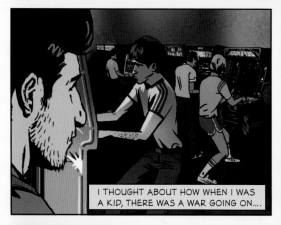

I THOUGHT ABOUT HOW WHEN I WAS A KID, THERE WAS A WAR GOING ON....

...AND EVERYTHING HAD COME TO A HALT.

THE FATHERS WERE ALL AWAY ON THE FRONT LINE.

THE CHILDREN STAYED INDOORS WITH THEIR MOTHERS...

...WAITING FOR A PLANE TO FLY OVER AND DROP A BOMB ON EVERYONE.

NOW, NO ONE SEEMED TO PUT THEIR LIFE ON HOLD, AND I WAS KIND OF THE SAME WAY.

I HAD ONLY ONE THOUGHT IN MY HEAD AT THE TIME.

AND THAT WAS TO GET MY GIRLFRIEND YAELI BACK.

SHE'D BROKEN UP WITH ME JUST BEFORE THE WHOLE THING HAD STARTED.

THINGS ARE STARTING TO COME BACK TO ME. I'VE GOT ALMOST THE WHOLE PICTURE...THE FIRST DAY OF THE WAR, THE SIEGE OF BEIRUT, THE FIRST TIME I CAME HOME

YOU REMEMBER YAELI HAD JUST DUMPED YOU?

HOW COME YOU REMEMBER THAT?

YOU KNOW, I WAS ALSO IN LOVE WITH HER FOR YEARS.

TO TELL YOU THE TRUTH, NO, I DIDN'T KNOW. NO.

WHAT'S THE MATTER? ARE YOU MAD AT ME? IT WAS MORE THAN TWENTY YEARS AGO.

LISTEN, AT LEAST YOU HAD YOUR HOME, YOUR FAMILY.

MY FAMILY? ARE YOU KIDDING? YOU KNOW WHAT MY DAD SAID TO COMFORT ME?

HE TOLD ME THAT IN HIS WAR, WORLD WAR II, THE RUSSIAN SOLDIERS AT STALINGRAD GOT FORTY-EIGHT HOURS' LEAVE AFTER A WHOLE YEAR AT THE FRONT.

THEY GOT ON A TRAIN, CAME INTO THE STATION, STEPPED OUT ON THE PLATFORM, AND KISSED THEIR WIVES AND GIRLFRIENDS.

THEN THEY BOARDED THE SAME TRAIN AND WENT STRAIGHT BACK TO THE FRONT.

AMAZINGLY, HE THOUGHT THAT WOULD MAKE ME FEEL BETTER. AND THEN, JUST AS IN HIS STORY, TWENTY-FOUR HOURS AFTER I WENT OUT ON LEAVE, THEY CALLED ME BACK. A NEW THING HAD STARTED, CAR BOMBS.

THERE WAS AN OFFICER SITTING IN A CHAIR IN FRONT OF THE TV. HE DIDN'T LOOK AT ME, HE TALKED TO HIS DRIVER.

GO FORWARD.
GO FORWARD.

WHILE THE DRIVER WAS PUSHING THE BUTTONS, THE OFFICER SAID TO ME:

LISTEN, WE GOT A HOT TIP.

A RED MERCEDES IS GOING TO EXPLODE ON YOUR MEN. SO WHEN THE CAR COMES, BLOW IT UP.

EVERY RED MERCEDES?

ARE YOU SOME KIND OF IDIOT OR WHAT?

SO WE WAITED ALL NIGHT, WATCHING FOR THE MERCEDES...

...EXPECTING SOME DREADFUL DISASTER.

AND THEN, JUST BEFORE DAWN, THE PHONE RANG.

I DON'T REMEMBER MUCH ABOUT THE FLIGHT TO WEST BEIRUT.

I HAD THESE OBSESSIVE THOUGHTS ABOUT DEATH...

...BECAUSE YAELI HAD LEFT ME.

ALL I WANTED WAS TO DIE, JUST TO GET BACK AT HER.

SO SHE'D BE LEFT WITH THE GUILT...

...FOR THE REST OF HER LIFE.

WHILE I WAS STILL FANTASIZING ABOUT DEATH, WE FLEW IN OVER BEIRUT, A BEAUTIFUL CITY WITH A BEACH, HOTELS.

WE LANDED AT THE INTERNATIONAL AIRPORT.

THERE WERE PASSENGER PLANES EVERYWHERE, AIR FRANCE, TWA, BRITISH AIRWAYS.

AND I FELT FULL OF EXCITEMENT, LIKE I WAS GOING ON VACATION.

AT SOME POINT I BROKE AWAY AND WENT UP TO THE TERMINAL.

I FOUND MYSELF ON A KIND OF TRIP, LIKE I WAS HALLUCINATING...

...AS THOUGH I REALLY WAS IN AN INTERNATIONAL AIRPORT.

ALL I HAD TO DO WAS CHOOSE, DECIDE ON A DESTINATION.

I STOOD IN FRONT OF THE DEPARTURES BOARD AND SAID TO MYSELF, OKAY, JUST CHOOSE.

I COULD TAKE THE 14:10 TO LONDON, THE 15:20 TO PARIS, THE 16:00 TO NEW YORK.

I CARRIED ON WANDERING AROUND THE TERMINAL...

...LOOKING AT THE DUTY FREE SHOPS, THE JEWELRY, TOBACCO, ALCOHOL.

AND WHILE I WAS STILL DEEP IN THIS TRIP...

...I SUDDENLY BEGAN TO GRASP WHAT WAS HAPPENING.

THROUGH THE WINDOWS, I COULD SEE THAT THE TWA AND AIR FRANCE PLANES OUTSIDE HAD BEEN BLOWN UP.

THEY WERE NOTHING BUT SKELETONS.

THE STORES—THEY WERE EMPTY.

THEY'D BEEN LOOTED A LONG TIME AGO.

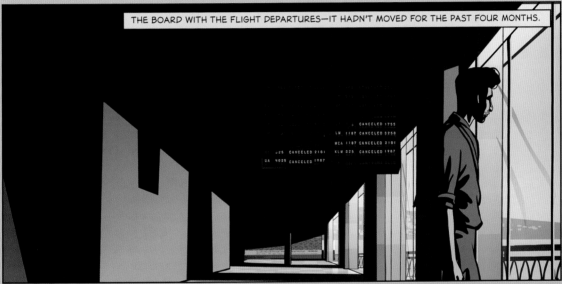

THE BOARD WITH THE FLIGHT DEPARTURES—IT HADN'T MOVED FOR THE PAST FOUR MONTHS.

THEN I STARTED HEARING THE SOUNDS, THE SHELLING IN THE CITY, THE AIR FORCE DROPPING BOMBS. I BEGAN TO TAKE IN WHERE I WAS.

AND I FELT SCARED OF WHAT WAS ABOUT TO HAPPEN.

WE WERE WALKING ALONG A KIND OF PROMENADE GOING TOWARD A BIG INTERSECTION. WE HAD NO WAY OF TELLING WHO WAS A SNIPER...

...AND WHO WAS A MUSICIAN.

THEN, SUDDENLY, THE SNIPERS STARTED, FIRING DOWN ON US FROM THE HOTELS.

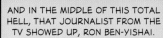

WE WERE SCARED OUT OF OUR MINDS.

AND IN THE MIDDLE OF THIS TOTAL HELL, THAT JOURNALIST FROM THE TV SHOWED UP, RON BEN-YISHAI.

HE WAS STRIDING THROUGH THE BULLETS, TALL, UPRIGHT, SUPERMAN, WALKING AS IF THERE WAS NOTHING GOING ON.

THE BULLETS WERE DOING ZIG-ZAGS OVER HIS HEAD, AND JUST IN FRONT OF HIM THERE WAS A CAMERAMAN, SHAKING WITH FEAR, CRAWLING ON ALL FOURS, BLINDED BY HIS HELMET.

RON BEN-YISHAI, ISRAEL'S GREATEST WAR CORRESPONDENT, HADN'T FORGOTTEN THE MADNESS THAT DAY ON HAMRA STREET.

THERE WAS A TREMENDOUS HISSING SOUND. THEY WERE FIRING MASSES OF RPGS, LIKE IN A SHOOTING RANGE. BEFORE THEY EXPLODE, AS THEY COME OVER, THE RPGS MAKE THIS WHIZZING NOISE, AND THERE'S THE PING OF THE SHELLS RICOCHETING OFF THE WALLS.

AND WITH ALL THIS GOING ON, THERE WERE CIVILIANS, STANDING OUT ON THEIR BALCONIES—WOMEN, CHILDREN, OLD PEOPLE, WATCHING AS IF THEY WERE AT A MOVIE.

SURE, I REMEMBER THE INTERSECTION. THEY WERE SHOOTING AT US FROM EVERY DIRECTION. THERE WAS NO WAY WE WERE GOING TO GET ACROSS THAT STREET.

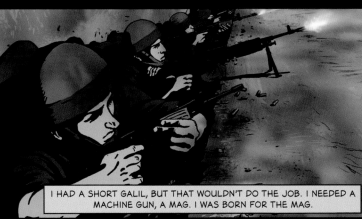

I HAD A SHORT GALIL, BUT THAT WOULDN'T DO THE JOB. I NEEDED A MACHINE GUN, A MAG. I WAS BORN FOR THE MAG.

EREZ, DO ME A FAVOR, GIVE ME THE MAG. I WON'T MAKE IT ACROSS OTHERWISE.

FRENKEL, ARE YOU CRAZY? THEY'RE SHOOTING AT US! SHUT UP AND SHOOT!

I KNEW I HAD TO DO SOMETHING DRAMATIC.

WE WEREN'T GOING TO GET OUT OF THERE OTHERWISE.

...JUST TO SHOW THEM: A WALTZ AMONG THEIR BULLETS.

AS FRENKEL DANCED BENEATH THE EYES OF THE SLAIN LEADER, BASHIR'S FOLLOWERS, NOT 200 YARDS FROM US, WERE PREPARING THEIR GREAT REVENGE: THE MASSACRES IN SABRA AND SHATILA.

IT WAS A JUNKYARD WHERE THEY TOOK THE PALESTINIANS TO INTERROGATE THEM. THEN THEY MURDERED THEM.

THAT PLACE WAS LIKE AN ACID TRIP. THEY KEPT BODY PARTS OF THE PALESTINIANS THEY'D KILLED IN JARS OF FORMALDEHYDE.

YOU COULD SEE FINGERS INSIDE A JAR, EYES, YOU NAME IT.

THE PHALANGISTS ALWAYS HAD PICTURES OF BASHIR ON THEM. BASHIR PENDANTS, BASHIR WATCHES, BASHIR THIS, BASHIR THAT.

THE MAN WAS THEIR IDOL, THEIR SUPERSTAR.

WHAT THEY FELT FOR HIM WAS EROTIC.

AND JUST BEFORE THEIR IDOL IS ABOUT TO BE CROWNED KING, HE'S MURDERED.

IT WAS OBVIOUS THEY'D AVENGE HIS DEATH IN A TOTALLY SICK WAY.

LISTEN, ORI, I'VE REACHED A DEAD END. I CAN'T FIND ANYONE WHO WAS WITH ME DURING THE MASSACRE.

I CAN'T FIND A SINGLE GENUINE MEMORY OF ANYONE CONNECTED TO ME THEN. THE ONLY THING I HAVE IS THE HALLUCINATION.

AND THE ONE PERSON WHO'S IN IT WITH ME DENIES ANY POSSIBILITY OF BEING THERE.

BUT YOUR HALLUCINATION IS REAL, IT'S YOURS. YOU WANT ME TO EXPLAIN IT TO YOU? IN DREAMS THE SEA SYMBOLIZES FEAR, FEELINGS. THE MASSACRE FRIGHTENS YOU. YOU BRUSHED UP AGAINST IT.

FOR YOU, THE SIGNIFICANCE OF THE MASSACRE WAS SET LONG BEFORE THE ACTUAL EVENT. IT COMES FROM A DIFFERENT MASSACRE. IT'S ABOUT WHAT HAPPENED IN THE OTHER CAMPS, THOSE CAMPS.

YOUR PARENTS WERE IN AUSCHWITZ, RIGHT? THE MASSACRE'S BEEN WITH YOU SINCE YOU WERE, I DON'T KNOW, SIX YEARS OLD.

YOUR ONLY WAY OUT IS TO LEARN WHAT REALLY HAPPENED IN SABRA AND SHATILA. TALK TO PEOPLE, FIND OUT HOW IT HAPPENED, WHO WAS WHERE. GET THE DETAILS.

THEY MIGHT LEAD YOU TO REMEMBER WHERE YOU WERE AND HOW YOU'RE CONNECTED TO IT.

ON THE DAY THE MASSACRES BEGAN, DROR HARAZI WAS STATIONED ON THE FRONT LINE WITH HIS TANK UNIT, RIGHT OUTSIDE THE REFUGEE CAMPS.

THEY SENT US TO A CERTAIN POST. IT WAS MORE LIKE A HILL, OVERLOOKING THE WESTERN PART OF THE CAMPS.

FROM MY POSITION I COULD SEE A RESIDENTIAL AREA, HOUSES.

EVERY NOW AND THEN THE PALESTINIANS FIRED AT US. WE'D TRY TO LOCATE THE SOURCE OF THE FIRE AND RETALIATE.

MEANWHILE, THE PHALANGIST FORCES GRADUALLY STARTED ARRIVING.

THEY WERE GOING IN TO PURGE THE
CAMPS OF PALESTINIAN TERRORISTS.

AND WE WERE THEIR COVER.

AFTER THAT, WE'D TAKE CONTROL.

ALL NIGHT WE HEARD SHOOTING FROM THE CAMPS, AND THE SKY WAS LIT WITH FLARES.

THE NEXT MORNING THEY STARTED BRINGING OUT THE CIVILIANS.

A LONG ROW OF PEOPLE WAS LED OUT OF THE CAMPS BY THE PHALANGISTS.

THERE WERE WOMEN, OLD PEOPLE, CHILDREN, ALL MOVING SLOWLY IN A LINE TOWARD THE CITY STADIUM.

THE PHALANGISTS KEPT SCREAMING AT THEM AND FIRING SHOTS IN THE AIR.

FROM OUR HILLTOP, WE SAW A PHALANGIST SOLDIER LEADING AN OLD MAN INTO A BUILDING.

WE HEARD SHOTS, A PUK-PUK-PUK SOUND.

THEN THE SOLDIER CAME OUT ALONE. WE CALLED DOWN TO HIM.

WHAT HAPPENED?

HE STARTED MOTIONING. HE'D TOLD THE MAN TO KNEEL DOWN. | WHEN THE MAN REFUSED, HE SHOT HIM IN THE KNEES... | ...THEN IN THE STOMACH, AND FINALLY... | ...IN HIS HEAD.

WAS THERE A MOMENT WHEN YOU PUT EVERYTHING TOGETHER, WHEN YOU TOLD YOURSELF: TRUCKS ARE GOING IN EMPTY, COMING OUT PACKED. WOMEN AND CHILDREN ARE LEAVING THE CAMP. THERE'S A BULLDOZER GOING IN. COULD THIS BE A MASSACRE?

YES, OF COURSE. BUT THAT ONLY HAPPENED AT THE POINT WHEN MY MEN SAID, "WE SAW IT."

THEY WERE SITTING ON TOP OF THE TANK.

SUDDENLY THEY SHRIEKED, "THEY JUST SHOT PEOPLE!"

MY MEN CLAIMED THEY SAW THE PHALANGISTS STAND PEOPLE UP AGAINST A WALL AND KILL THEM.

THAT'S WHEN I CALLED MY COMMANDING OFFICER DIRECTLY. I TOLD HIM ABOUT ACTIVITIES GOING ON IN THE CAMPS. HE SAID, "WE KNOW, IT'S UNDER CONTROL, WE'VE REPORTED IT." SO AS FAR AS I WAS CONCERNED, THE ISRAELI ARMY KNEW ABOUT IT AND WAS DEALING WITH IT.

THE COMMAND CENTER WAS LOCATED BEHIND US, ABOUT ONE HUNDRED YARDS AWAY, ON TOP OF A VERY TALL BUILDING WHERE THEY COULD LOOK DOWN AND SEE EVERYTHING. THEY PROBABLY HAD A BETTER VIEW THAN I DID.

ON THE DAY OF THE MASSACRE, RON BEN-YISHAI WAS ON HIS WAY TO DOHA, A PLACE BY THE SEA.

I WAS DRIVING TO THE ARMY'S LANDING FIELD THERE.

ON THE ROADS I NOTICED A LOT OF PHALANGISTS. THEY WERE VERY HAPPY, LIVELY.

I JUST CONTINUED ON MY WAY.

I DIDN'T LIKE WALKING AROUND BEIRUT AT NIGHT.

SO I WENT BACK TO MY APARTMENT AND HAD SOME GUYS OVER FOR DINNER.

THEY WERE FROM A REGIMENT IN THE 211TH BRIGADE. THE REGIMENT COMMANDER TOOK ME ASIDE.

RON, MY MEN SAY THERE'S A MASSACRE GOING ON IN THE CAMPS. THEY SAW A FAMILY TAKEN OUT AND SHOT. I DIDN'T SEE IT MYSELF, BUT MY SOLDIERS TOLD ME AND SO DID THE OFFICERS SITTING HERE.

ON THE FINAL DAY OF THE MASSACRE, I WAS UP AT ABOUT 5:00 OR 5:30.

I GOT MY TEAM AND DROVE TOWARD SABRA AND SHATILA.

WE ARRIVED THERE AND... WHAT A MESS.

YOU KNOW THE PICTURE OF THE WARSAW GHETTO? THE ONE OF THE BOY WITH HIS HANDS UP? A LONG TRAIN OF WOMEN, OLD PEOPLE, AND CHILDREN WERE WALKING LIKE THAT, WITH THEIR HANDS UP.

THIS WAS THE ACT THAT STOPPED THE MASSACRE. THE PHALANGISTS DISAPPEARED DOWN THE STREET, WHILE THE PALESTINIAN WOMEN AND CHILDREN TURNED BACK TO THE CAMP.

WE WENT IN WITH THEM TO SEE WHAT WAS HAPPENING. INSIDE THE CAMP I SAW A HUGE AMOUNT OF RUBBLE.

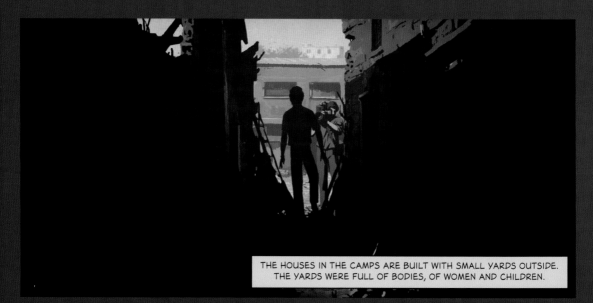

THE HOUSES IN THE CAMPS ARE BUILT WITH SMALL YARDS OUTSIDE.
THE YARDS WERE FULL OF BODIES, OF WOMEN AND CHILDREN.

FIRST THEY TOOK THE YOUNG MEN AND SHOT THEM.

THEN THEY SETTLED ACCOUNTS WITH THE FAMILIES.

WE WENT INTO A NARROW ALLEY, ABOUT THE WIDTH OF A MAN AND A HALF. THE ALLEY WAS BLOCKED, TO ABOUT CHEST HEIGHT, WITH THE BODIES OF YOUNG MEN.

AND THEN IT CAME OVER ME: WHAT I WAS LOOKING AT WAS A MASSACRE.

Acknowledgments

This book owes its existence to Riva Hocherman at Metropolitan Books. Her initiative, insight, and patient guidance helped shape every aspect of its creation. Thanks are due to Yoni Goodman, director of animation for the film *Waltz with Bashir,* who developed the movie's storyboards. The illustrations here took their cue from his essential work. Our thanks as well to Asaf Hanuka, Michael Faust, Tomer Hanuka, and Yaara Buchman, part of the film's illustration team, whose drawings are included in this book. Roi Baron assisted the book's production in ways large and small. Finally, grateful acknowledgment is made to Robin Moyer for use of his photographs of the massacre in the Sabra and Shatila refugee camps.

About the Authors

ARI FOLMAN, a Tel Aviv–based filmmaker, wrote, produced, and directed the animated documentary *Waltz with Bashir*. His previous two feature films, *Saint Clara* and *Made in Israel*, won numerous Israeli academy awards, among them Best Film and Best Director for *Saint Clara*, which also received the People's Choice Award at the 1996 Berlin Film Festival. In addition, Ari Folman produces and writes for television, including for the Israeli series *In Treatment*, which was remade in the United States for HBO.

DAVID POLONSKY was art director and chief illustrator for the animated film *Waltz with Bashir*. His illustrations have appeared in every major Israeli daily and magazine. He has created animated short films for television, received multiple awards for his children's book illustrations, and teaches illustration at Bezalel, Israel's prestigious art academy.